The English Lakes

The Hills, The People, Their History

(an illustrated walking guide, complete with local history)

Book Three - The Helvellyn Range

by David Ramshaw

Line Drawings by
David Lush

Relief Map by
John Adams

This Book is dedicated to Frances

The English Lakes
The Hills, The People, Their History
(an illustrated walking guide, complete with local history)
Book 3: The Helvellyn Range

In 1994 David Ramshaw and John Adams published a book of the same title which covered the whole of the Lake District National Park; splitting it up into eight different areas. The walking and local history sections of the original book have been revised and brought up to date by David Ramshaw and the format has been changed. It was decided to publish the new edition of the work as a series of pocket sized books, each of which cover a different area of the district.
This is the third of the new pocket editions. The area covered by this book is shown on the relief map on the back cover.

David Ramshaw has asserted his right under the Copyright, Designs and Patents Act 1988 to be identified as the author of this work.

Copyright © David Ramshaw 2002

British Library Cataloguing In Publication Data
A catalogue record for this book is available from the British Library
Second Edition published in Great Britain in 2002 by:

ISBN 0 9537203 5 7

P3 Publications
13 Beaver Road
Carlisle
Cumbria
CA2 7PS

Printed in Great Britain by
Amadeus Press
Cleckheaton
BD19 4TQ

The Helvellyn Range
Useful Information

Access and Country Code -
The description of a route in this book does not necessarily imply a right of way. Please respect the country code. **DO NOT** climb over or damage walls, fences or hedges. **DO NOT** deposit litter, take it home with you. Take care not to frighten livestock. **DO** follow marked paths wherever possible, using stiles and gates. **DO** close gates after you and **DO** keep your dog under close control, **ON A LEAD** (if he is not fully trained to stay by you and completely ignore sheep).

On the Hills: it is essential that anyone intending to venture onto the hills is properly equipped for the conditions that they may encounter. The following items of equipment are, in our opinion, the minimum necessary for a fine weather trip onto the Lakeland Fells:

Strong walking boots, woollen trousers or breeches (not cotton jeans), windproof anorak with hood, spare sweater, gloves, extra emergency food, first aid kit, map, compass, torch, whistle, a survival bag and of course a rucksack to put them all in.

More information: a free leaflet is available, from the Information and Visitor Centres throughout the National Park, entitled Safety on the Fells.

The proximity of the lakeland mountains to the Irish Sea and the prevailing westerly winds can lead to sudden and dramatic changes in the weather. It is all too common to set out for the tops in warm and pleasant conditions to be confronted, sometime later, with driving rain and a cold blustery wind. Do **NOT** get caught out. Go properly equipped.

The National Park Ranger Service: provides a recorded fell top weather report, which is updated twice daily. The number to call is 017687 75757

The Helvellyn Range
Useful Information

In an emergency: If you are unlucky enough to get into difficulties and you have no phone, or no signal, use the international distress signal to attract attention. This consists of six blasts on a whistle, or six flashes of a torch, or six shouts. Wait one minute before repeating the signal. The reply to this signal is three blasts on a whistle, or three flashes of a torch, repeated at one minute intervals.

For mountain or mines rescue dial 999 and ask for Police who will contact the local rescue team. Please, only use the emergency services if you are in real need. Since the advent of mobile phones many unnecessary calls have been made to the emergency services by people who are not in any real danger.

Maps: The special relief maps in the book are included only to give a general indication of the route. Readers attempting the routes in this book are recommended to use a suitable walking map, such as the Ordnance Survey 1:25000 Outdoor Leisure Map for the English Lakes, North Western Area.

The start point of walks, places or path junctions are occasionally given a letter in the text e.g. quote from page 13:

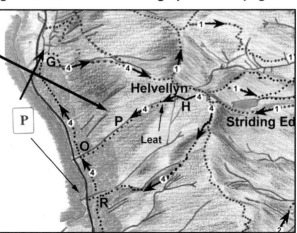

(a) Return by Brownrigg Well (H) and Helvellyn Mine (P)
These letters refer to points on the map on page 16.
This is an ideal route for the local history enthusiast, but it is also **a very steep descent into Mines Ghyll,** so only experienced hill walkers should tackle it. If unsure use **Return Route (b).**
From the trig. point on the summit of Helvellyn walk due west (compass bearing 276 magnetic) straight down the hillside for a distance of about 500 m. This should bring you to a noticeable depression, the source of a stream, which is a tributary of Whelpside Gill. Brownrigg Well is the name given to the spring which issues from the hillside here; providing pure clear water even in the longest drought **(LH8)**.
(LH8) refers to Local History item No. 8, which will be found in the Local History Section (See page 28).

The Helvellyn Range
General

Although not the highest, Helvellyn (The Hill of Willan) is probably the best known mountain in Lakeland. This is, I feel, more likely due to the attraction of the Striding and Swirral Edges than to its own grandeur. Helvellyn is the high point of a meandering ridge which rises in the north at Clough Head, traverses the Dodds and Raise to the rounded and rather featureless summit dome of Lakeland's second highest mountain. From here the ridge continues south over Nethermost and Dollywaggon Pikes, dropping briefly to Grisedale Tarn, before rising to the stony summit of Fairfield. A gentle descent over Rydal Fell then follows until valley level is reached once more at Rydal Water.

This line of mountains can be thought of as the backbone of the Lake District running north to south and separating east from west. Accordingly, they form a fine platform from which to enjoy the beauties of the area. To the west the ground generally drops steeply down to the vales of Grasmere and Thirlmere, giving limited and rather unremarkable access to the tops. In contrast, on the eastern side many subsidiary ridges fall away in a north easterly direction towards the vales containing Ullswater and Brotherswater. These ridges enclose rocky coves and narrow passes, which eventually become picturesque green valleys as they descend to the hamlets of Matterdale, Dockray, Glenridding, Patterdale and Hartsop. Consequently access to the ridge is easier, more varied and more scenic from the east. However, there are many steep crags and rocky precipices to the east of the summit ridge and care must be taken in poor visibility or winter conditions. Beware of cornices and ice beneath the snow on the ridges in winter. Many people over the years have taken the quick route to Red Tarn from the summit plateau, often with disastrous results.

> A serious young lady from Welwyn
> took a cookery book up Helvellyn.
> While reading the recipes
> She fell down a precipice,
> And that was the end of poor Ellen !
> Lakeland Limericks, Gibbs 1942

The valleys ringing the Helvellyn range are rich in local history. There are stories of myth and legend in the early border battles. There are tales of the lives of the lake poets; who did so much to popularise and romanticise the Lake District in the early nineteenth century. Finally there is the influence of industry on the people and the landscape. The remains of lead and iron mines still scar the fells, silent reminders of once thriving industries which, before the age of tourism, were the lifeblood of the district. The water industry, in the guise of Manchester Corporation, has also left its mark, (still to be seen in a drought), with the creation of the Thirlmere reservoir during the last quarter of the nineteenth century.

Red Tarn and Helvellyn, from the approach to Striding Edge

The Helvellyn Range
Walking

All grades and lengths of walks can be found in this area. There are several rounds or horseshoe routes which follow the high ridges as well as two ancient packhorse tracks crossing east to west through narrow passes. Apart from these higher paths, there are many delightful family walks around the foothills. These can be found in Matterdale, Gowbarrow Park and Glencoyne to the east, as well as Grasmere, White Moss Common and Rydal to the south. Because of the profusion of paths and possible routes, only a selection of walks will be described. The reader is invited to use the maps to plan alternative ascents and descents. **The maps, to which the text refers, are to be found on the centre pages of the book.**

Walks from Glenridding and Patterdale

Route 1 - Helvellyn via Striding Edge

(a)   Return via Swirral Edge, Total climbing about 2630 ft (802 m), 7 miles (11 km).

(b)   Return via Lower Man, White Side and Greenside Mine. Total climbing about 2830 ft (863 m), 10 miles (16 km).

  This classic round must be one of the most popular in Lakeland. There is only limited parking on the road leading into Grisedale; one possible start point. If there is no room you must park either at Glenridding **(L)** or at Patterdale **(N)**. If parking at Glenridding then follow the alternative route (ii) up to Striding Edge.

(i) Starting from the Grisedale Road (N)

  Follow the narrow road leading past the entrance to Patterdale Hall for about a quarter of a mile, when you will arrive at a gate barring vehicles from continuing up the valley. Turn right here for the well worn path which crosses the bridge over Grisedale Beck, before striking steeply up the side of Birkhouse Moor. The gradient soon eases as the route traverses the hillside arriving, in just over a mile, at The hole in the wall **(J)**, at the summit of Bleaberry Crag. There are two stiles giving access over the wall onto the Birkhouse Moor ridge.

(ii) Starting from Glenridding car park and Visitor Centre (L)

Cross to the minor road along the south side of Glenridding Beck by the bridge on the main road and follow it westwards past the tea rooms, the shops and the village hall. In about 200m you will see a wooden signpost indicating Lanty s Tarn **(M)** and Helvellyn, up the hill and   Bridleway Gillside, Miresbeck, Greenside, Helvellyn straight on. This latter route is the more direct for Helvellyn. Follow it past Gillside campsite to meet the track from Rattlebeck Bridge **(LH4)** just south of the bridge. Continue south (Signpost Helvellyn via Miresbeck, 3 miles) for a further 200m to reach a path junction (Signpost Lanty 's Tarn to the left). Turn right here onto a broad rough track which, in a further 150m brings you to a gate, the open fell and a path junction. Turn left and ascend the well made path which leads up Miresbeck onto the Birkhouse Moor ridge at point **(K)** on the map. You can now recover your breath as you stroll southwest towards Helvellyn and Striding Edge

The Helvellyn Range
Walking

Soon Striding Edge will appear before you with Red Tarn to the right, nestling under the massive northern face of Helvellyn and the steep-sided Swirral Edge. A splendid view at any time, this scene is especially majestic when bedecked by winter snows, (see the drawing on page 5). As you come on to the edge proper the view down to your left is spectacular. The dark northern face of St. Sunday's Crag looms ominously above the narrow green strip of the Grisedale Valley as it pushes between its two enclosing mountains. The edge itself is an engrossing rocky scramble, quite safe in good conditions, but obviously to be avoided in high winds or when icy. As you cross the edge look for the white memorial plaque commemorating an accidental death in 1858 **(LH6)**. At the end of the edge an interesting rock chimney descent of about twenty feet marks

the start of the final pull up to the rounded summit of Helvellyn, which is endowed with two more memorials **(LH6);** a stone wall shelter and an O.S. trig. point. The views to the east are the most delightful to the eye, with Red Tarn immediately below and Ullswater stretching away in the background.

(a) Return via Swirral Edge

To return by Swirral Edge follow the ridge path north keeping close to the edge above Red Tarn so as not to miss the path leading onto Swirral Edge. The descent of Swirral Edge must be taken with care. The path, although quite good, is loose in places and some of the boulders are very large. To the left the ground drops away down into Brown Cove, with Keppel Cove and its dried up tarn and broken dams beyond; the cause of the great flood of Glenridding earlier this century **(LH4)**. High up in the cove can be seen the spoil heaps of Brown Cove Mine; a small lead working, which was probably part of the immensely successful Greenside Mine complex **(LH3)**.

Eventually the route along Swirral Edge starts to climb up again towards the summit of Catstycam. The name Catstycam or Catchedecam has interesting origins. According to McIntyre it is probably a corruption of Cat-steg-cam, the steg (mountain ladder or path) of the wild cats. Although this was the haunt of wild cats in days gone by it is unlikely that they inhabit the area now. Our path, however, drops away down to Red Tarn, crossing close by the dam at its northern corner and climbing to rejoin the path of ascent at the summit of Bleaberry Crag.

Striding Edge from Helvellyn top

The Helvellyn Range
Walking

(b) Return via Lower Man, White Side and Greenside (taking you back to Glenridding).

From the summit of Helvellyn follow the main path, which descends gently to the northwest, as far as Lower Man, just at the end of the summit plateau. As you descend don't forget to look back for a splendid view of the northwestern side of Swirral Edge as it drops away from the summit ridge (see drawing below).

At Lower Man the path splits. This is a good viewpoint for gazing down into the depths of Brown Cove. The erratic rocky terrain, with Swirral Edge rising on the right, forms a dramatic picture. One arm of the path continues in a northwesterly direction, as it drops steeply down over the reddish brown rocks of Brown Cove Crags towards the road at The Swirls car park **(G)**. We must follow the other arm as it meanders north along the ridge above Keppel Cove, eventually climbing to the summit of White Side. From White Side the path contours east above Red Screes before zig zagging down between the crags into the lower reaches of Keppel Cove. This area is littered with the signs of old mine workings. There are water leats, an old dam, a weir and an old pipeline as well as several spoil heaps and old levels. In the heyday of Greenside Mine this was the catchment area for the water needed to provide electric power for the winding gear and eventually for an electric locomotive. The large concrete dam with the hole in the base was not responsible for the great flood of Glenridding mentioned earlier. The dam which caused the flood is the smaller earth dam behind it at the southern end of the now dry Keppelcove Tarn. If you climb to the top, note how it was constucted of waste products from the mine site. In particular the reinforcing rods protruding from the concrete consist of discarded drill bits. They are the more modern type with a hole down the middle through which high pressure water was squirted to keep down the dust. The route now continues northeast, just to the north of the Glenridding Beck; which wends its way down through the mine buildings at Greenside. These now house Helvellyn Youth Hostel and several outdoor activity centres. The mine road can now be followed down to Glenridding village. As you descend note the old explosives building, the landscaped spoil heaps and the rows of miners cottages, all reminders of a bygone age.

Swirral Edge in Winter, seen from the path to Lower Man

The Helvellyn Range
Walking

Route 2 - Fairfield via St. Sunday Crag

     (a) Return via Grisedale. Total Climbing about 2900 ft (884 m), 8 miles (13 km).
     (b) Return via Hart Crag. Total Climbing about 3030 ft (924 m), 9 miles (14.5 km)

The start point for this walk is the same as for **Route 1**. Take the road into Grisedale as before and, in about a quarter of a mile, a gate in the wall marks the start of the path up onto Thornhow End **(Q)**. This leads across a field before climbing quite steeply up onto the ridge of Birks. Here the gradient eases a little, giving some relief before the pull up to the summit of St Sunday Crag. On a fine day this is a fine place to rest and idly count the ants in the distance as they creep across Striding Edge. At least you are more likely to have the summit of St Sunday Crag to yourself than you are the summit of Helvellyn.

    Continuing on, we must first descend about 150m to Deepdale Hause before encountering the steep rocky scramble on to Cofa Pike, which leads up to the broad rock and grass summit of Fairfield itself **(S)**. There are good views to be had in all directions from the summit plateau of Fairfield and in clear still conditions it is a pleasant place to be. Unfortunately, in my experience, it is more likely to be windy, wet and covered in cloud. There are four main routes of Fairfield, which are all quite obvious in clear weather, but finding them can be difficult in mist. Care needs to be taken in these conditions as there are steep crags to the east above Deepdale.

(a) Return via Grisedale (Norse: grys dale, the valley of the pigs)
The path down to Grisedale Tarn leads off due west from the summit cairn above the crags, dropping steeply down to Grisedale Hause. Turn north at the hause and join the ancient pack horse route which connects Grasmere to Patterdale. The track fords Grisedale Beck at the point where it leaves Grisedale Tarn.

The Brothers Parting Stone

Grisedale Tarn features in the legend of King Dunmail **(LH5)** who supposedly lost his life in the battle of Dunmail Raise. Just past the tarn, on the descent into Grisedale, look for the inscribed brothers parting stone made famous by William Wordsworth's poem in which he laments the loss of his brother John **(LH10)**.

The Helvellyn Range
Walking

The Grisedale track descends the northern side of the valley as far as Ruthwaite Lodge climbing hut; an old mine building. Here the main track crosses Grisedale Beck to the south side of the valley. There are two lead mines here in Grisedale, Ruthwaite Lodge and, a little further on, the larger Eagle Crag Mine. Both are ancient dating back to Elizabethan times. Neither has been worked since 1880. Eagle Crag Mine can be seen at close quarters if you continue along the track on the north side of the valley for a further half mile, before crossing to the south side of the beck. To return to the start point continue down the track, which gradually improves, until it becomes a road at Elmhow farmhouse; now an outdoor centre.

(b) Return via Hart Crag (the crag of the deer)

This route takes us from the summit of Fairfield (**S**), across the hause above Rydal Head to Hart Crag. In fine weather this is no problem but be careful in mist. From the summit cairn you must walk in a southeasterly direction. Keep the edge of the ridge, on your left, in view, so as not to miss the path across the hause. About two hundred metres from the cairn you should encounter the Hart Crag path which strikes off almost due east. In mist keep to the south side of the hause just above Rydal Head as there are steep crags on the northern side. Cairns mark the summit of Hart Crag (**T**) and the return path descends in a northeasterly direction to the Hartsop Above How ridge.

As you descend on to the ridge look for the Priest's Hole Cave; a large rectangular slot high on the face of Dove Crag; the rocky outcrop southeast of Hart Crag. The Priest Hole is about twenty feet across and about ten feet deep. A small wall across the entrance serves to dissuade sheep from entering. The cave is often used by groups of walkers, or climbers on Dove Crag, as an overnight shelter. If you decide to spend the night there don't forget to record the event in the visitor book which is kept in the tin box inside the cave. The path up to the cave is a rocky scramble from the cove beneath but is well worth the effort. The outlook from the Priest Hole can only be described as an "Eagle's Eye View. It is an unforgettable experience early on a frosty spring morning, when the rising sun cuts through the mist to burn you out of your sleeping bag. The name of the cave probably dates back to the Civil War and religious persecution, although I have found no written evidence for this. The route back to Patterdale follows the long curve of the Hartsop Above How ridge, which descends to Deepdale Bridge on the Patterdale-Kirkstone Pass road. The road must now be followed back into Patterdale where liquid refreshment is generally available.

Low level walks around Glenridding

For those wishing to get a taste of the high places without climbing too high there are many paths not rising much more than 700 ft above valley level. A network of such paths criss-cross the lower slopes of Birkhouse Moor in the area of Lanty's Tarn. These routes link Grisedale with the Glenridding valley and are ideal for family walks on a fine day.

The Helvellyn Range
Walking

For a longer expedition follow the path to Greenside Mine; which contours along the southern side of the Glenridding valley at a height of about 1000 ft above sea level. This route provides splendid views of the valley, the old lead workings, with the hills beyond and, if we look back, Glenridding village and Ullswater. To return just follow the mine road down the northside of the valley.

Gowbarrow Park and Aira Force

This National Trust area has adequate parking (free if you are a member) and a network of well maintained paths which meander through the woods leading to the spectacular Aira Force waterfall **(D)**. The main fall is a vertical drop of 70 ft. and is well worth seeing when in spate. For those who would find difficulty climbing up to the height of the falls from the Ullswater road car park there is limited waiting parking; two hours, opposite the falls on the Matterdale road. If the weather is fine one can venture up on to Gowbarrow Fell or Park; an ideal viewpoint for seeing all of the reaches of Ullswater. A pleasant walk can be had from Gowbarrow which follows the low meandering ridge above Swinburn's Park as far as the road, a mile west of Watermillock.

Route 3 A circular walk from Dockray - Total climbing about 1500 ft (457 m).
Return via Dowthwaitehead 7.5 miles (12 km)

This route which, takes the walker to about 2480 ft above sea level with relatively gentle gradients, is ideal for a fine lazy day. It also offers more peace and solitude than many other paths in the vicinity. However, a word of warning is necessary. The inexperienced fellwalker will find no difficulty with these routes in clear weather, when reading the map is easy. In mist however, these lower fells are often more confusing than their larger relatives. The summits are rounded, dotted with hillocks, covered in vegetation and often swampy in places. As a result the paths can disappear and reappear, split and rejoin, get confused with sheeptracks etc.. Less experienced walkers, should only tackle these walks in relatively good weather. A final observation: when the weather is too bad for the high summits these lower routes can provide good map reading practice for the more experienced walker. There is a small parking area near the bridge in Dockray **(A)**. Take the track opposite, beside the green wooden hut, which leads through a gate onto Watermillock Common (National Trust sign). Do not follow the farm track which

Ruined Shooting Lodge, Gowbarrow Park
on the path towards Swinburn's Park

fords the stream but, keeping the stream on your right, strike off up the hillside towards the summit of Common Fell (SSW). There is no continuous discernible path in spite of the heavy dotted line across the 1:25000 map. These paths would be well used long ago by the early Greenside miners, tramping up to the head of the Glencoyne valley, but they are now barely visible. Keep to the left of the summit and you will arrive at a drystone wall which marks the ridge path leading up from the old quarry on the Dockray road at Aira Force. There is now a good path to follow on the right of the wall which gives excellent views of Ullswater and Place Fell beyond. In about a mile the wall, and the path, contour round into the Glencoyne valley. The path here, being very broken and indistinct, is marked by the occasional small stone cairn. If you maintain your height and aim for the head of the valley the route soon reappears, leading on to the waste heap which marks the old Glencoyne level of Greenside Mine **(F)**. This was the goal of the early miners in the eighteenth century; who were responsible for the rights of way leading from here to the surrounding villages and hamlets. Below to your left, at the neck of the upper valley, note the old dam, now breached, which at one time stored water for use in the mine. This path, as it contours round under the crags below the summit of Hartside, leads one into the remote upper valley of Glencoynedale. The rugged aspect of the enclosing hills of Sheffield Pike and Stybarrow Dodd is more reminiscent of the remoter parts of the Scottish Highlands than the Lake District.

From the mine follow the path around the head of the valley as far as the hause between Sheffield Pike and Stybarrow Dodd. From here you can look down onto the old workings, walls and dams, which litter the floor of the valley between Raise and the Dodds. This valley is the route of the Sticks Pass path linking Glenridding to St. John's in the Vale. Note the ski hut and tow on the north side of Raise; which retains snow longer than most other places in the district. From the hause follow the old miners path which climbs north up the ridge above Glencoyne Head onto the rounded grassy top of Hart Side **(C)**. The deep trench dug east to west across the summit is a reminder of the last few years of mining at Greenside. The owners knew that the rich lead vein, on which the mine had been built, was finally running out. Exploratory work was carried out in the 1950's. Alas no further ore was found and the mine finally closed in 1962.

The Old Dam in Glencoynedale

The Helvellyn Range
Walking

From the top of Hart Side there is no discernible path so one must descend the grassy northern face on either side of Coegill Beck to the farm at Douthwaite Head **(B)**. Towards the bottom the route intersects a more direct miners path from the Glencoyne valley.As you approach the valley bottom look for the stiles over the drystone walls. Please do not attempt to climb over the walls. From Douthwaite Head a well marked path, (yellow arrows), signposted 'Footpath to Matterdale' crosses the fields almost midway between the road and Aira Beck. If you have a large dog use the road instead as there are several ladder stiles crossing drystone walls with no holes for dogs provided. This path eventually emerges on the Dockray road half a mile from the startpoint.

Helvellyn from the Thirlmere side

Helvellyn can be accessed from Thirlmere from either Grasmere, Dunmail Raise, Wythburn or The Swirls. The latter two routes offer short but rather steep paths to the summit.

Route 4 - Helvellyn from The Swirls. Total Climbing 2460 ft (750 m).
Return via (a) Brownrigg Well **(LH8)**, Helvellyn Mine and forest path. 5 miles (8 km).
　　　　　　 (b) Wythburn and forest path. 7 miles (11 km).

The startpoint of this walk is the car park at The Swirls **(G)**. Cross the bridge over the beck and follow the excellent path that leads southeast up the ridge to Brown Cove Crags and Helvellyn Lower Man. This is a steep and unremitting climb until Lower Man is reached, but it is the most direct route to the summit. The final kilometre from Lower Man to the Helvellyn top is a pleasant stroll.

(a) Return by Brownrigg Well (H) and Helvellyn Mine (P)

This is an ideal route for the local history enthusiast, but it is also **a very steep descent into Mines Ghyll,** so only experienced hill walkers should tackle it. If unsure use **Return Route (b).**

From the trig. point on the summit of Helvellyn walk due west (compass bearing 276 magnetic) straight down the hillside for a distance of about 500 m. This should bring you to a noticeable depression, the source of a stream, which is a tributary of Whelpside Gill. Brownrigg Well is the name given to the spring which issues from the hillside here; providing pure clear water even in the longest drought **(LH8)**. This stream was used by the miners of Helvellyn in the 19th century and the line of the old water leat, seen as a groove in the ground, can be followed northwards over into the narrow valley of Mines Ghyll. Follow the leat down into the valley to join the main stream, very steep in parts and no proper path. Once in the valley bottom a miners path leads one down through the old levels, past a dam and the ruins of the drum house, which controlled the tubs on the gravity operated incline; seen lower down. Lower down on the left are the remains of mine buildings **(P)**, a bothy and smithy (Note the drill holes in the stones near the door where the smith tested the drill after sharpening it). Justbeyond this point look for evidence of possibly the oldest and highest flush toilet in the country. A barely visible path leading contours west from the bothy to reach a small square of stones, situated over a (now dry) streambed. This is all that remains of the walls of an outside toilet with an exceptional view over Thirlmere. When operational in the late l9th century, water, flowing under the seat, would flush any waste down into Helvellyn Ghyll. A discernible path continues down the hill to the left of the stream. Note the remains of the gravity operated tub incline on the opposite bank. This was used to raise empty tubs and lower ones full with ore to the valley below. Towards the bottom of the hill the main path through the wood between Dunmail Raise and Swirls is reached. Here there is still evidence of the remains of a water powered ore crushing plant. To find out more about Wythburn Mine read the book of that title by Alen McFadzean (1987) or Thirlmere Mines, Ian Tyler (2001).

At the path junction (**O**) turn right and follow the woodland path back to Swirls Car Park.

(b) Return by Wythburn and forest path

From the summit of Helvellyn take the main path south towards Nethermost Pike. In 600m a path junction is reached. take the lower path which descends down the Birkside Ridge, slightly south of Comb Crags, before turning north and zig zagging steeply down to the woods above Wythburn Church. Shortly after entering the woods (where red squirrels can often be seen) the path crosses the woodland path between Dunmail Raise and Swirls (**R**). Turn right (northwards) onto this track to return to Swirls Car Park.

Clough Head and The Dodds

Access to these northern hills of the Helvellyn Range can be gentle and long from Matterdale in the east or short and steep from the Vale of St. John in the west. The Dodds, as their name suggests, consist of a group of rounded grassy summits on a high plateau. The tops are linked by a broad meandering ridge which starts at Clough Head and finishes at Sticks Pass.

Walking the Dodds

There is little to say about walking the Dodds. The terrain is rather unexciting, except in snow, but good views are to be had in all directions of the surrounding countryside. One can plan an interesting round from Douthwaite Head in Matterdale (**B**), which takes in some or all of the tops. Alternatively, one can ascend Clough Head from Bramcrag Quarry in St John's in the Vale and follow the ridge to Stick's Pass, which then affords a scenic descent to Sty Beck Farm (**E**). This latter route does involve rather a long road walk at the end unless you have two cars available.

The Helvellyn Range
Walking

Walks from Grasmere The beautiful village of Grasmere has, unfortunately, become a victim of its own fame. In the past it was an important centre of the wool and mining industries. Now it is the centre of the tourist industry and much of the peace, quiet and romance of the area, described by Wordsworth and others, has been destroyed by the influx of those seeking these very delights. However one can still scale the surrounding heights to escape the madding throng. One possible walk which takes in a fair amount of local history and legend is detailed below.

Route 5 Fairfield via Great Rigg

Return via Grisedale Tarn and Little Tongue Gill.
Total climbing about 2570 ft (784 m), 7 miles (11 km).

Grasmere in 1819 (from an old print)

Car parking is available in the village but it could be expensive depending on the time of year. The start point for the walk is the minor road which leads up to Greenhead Gill from the Swan Hotel. When you pass through the gate there is a choice of routes. The path to the left, between two walls, leads up onto Stone Arthur. This is the more scenic route to Great Rigg but it avoids the places of historical interest. If the gill is followed the walker can observe the concrete tunnel of the Thirlmere aqueduct, as is emerges from the hillside to cross this narrow valley **(LH7)**.

Further up, at the sharp bend in the gill, is an open adit or mine entrance. This is the Greenhead Gill trial, an exploratory venture, which was probably trying to access the vein of the Grasmere lead mine. This is found round the corner further up Greenhead Gill at it's junction with Grains Gill. Grasmere lead mine is ancient. A short lived venture, it was opened by the company of Mines Royal about 1564 and closed in 1573. Beyond the mine the gill is steep sided and rather an uninteresting ascent so, if you have come this way, a diversion to the right, which follows Grains Gill up onto the Rydal Fell ridge, might be preferred. However, this is a very steep route. If you would prefer to follow a path then backtrack to the bend in the gill and follow the steep track up onto Heron Pike. Having attained the ridge the remainder of the walk to the summit of Fairfield is a pleasant stroll, at a gentle rate of ascent.

The return route on the old pack horse track via Grisedale Tarn and Grisedale Hause leads one past the old Tongue Gill iron mines. These mines were first worked in the seventeenth century but were reopened in the early 1870's for a short time when the price of iron shot up, as a result of demand due to the Franco - Prussian war. Neither mine has been worked since 1876. The red staining on the ground, due to the haematite content, is very noticeable. It is not advisable to get it on your clothes.

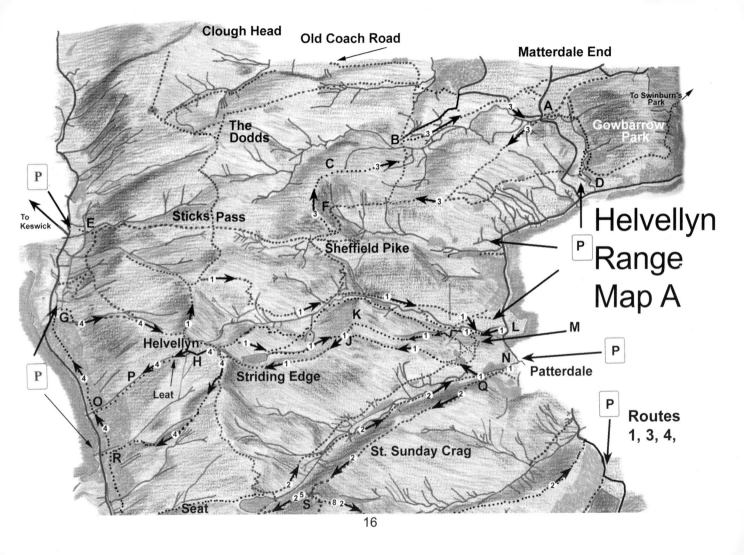

Clough Head

Old Coach Road

Matterdale End

To Swinburn's Park

Gowbarrow Park

A

3

3

B 3

3

C 3

D

F 3

3

To Keswick

E

Sticks Pass

Sheffield Pike

The Dodds

Helvellyn Range Map A

P

P

P

P

1

1

1

K

1

1

1 1 L

M

1 1 J 1

N

Patterdale

G 4 4 4

1

Helvellyn

4 4

H

4

Striding Edge

Q 1

P 4

Leat

O 4

4

R 4

2

2

2

St. Sunday Crag

2

P

Routes 1, 3, 4,

Seat 2 5 S 8 2

2

2

16

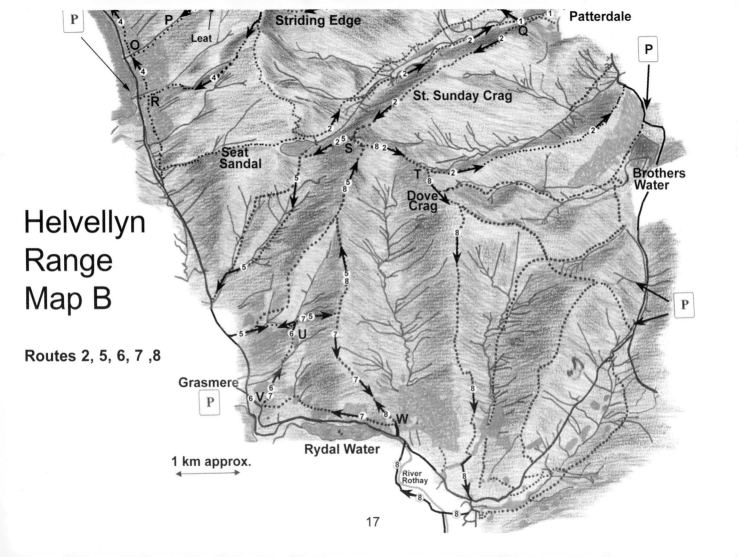

Helvellyn
Range
Map B

Routes 2, 5, 6, 7 ,8

Striding Edge

Leat

Patterdale

St. Sunday Crag

Brothers
Water

Seat
Sandal

Dove
Crag

Grasmere

Rydal Water

River
Rothay

1 km approx.

The Helvellyn Range
Walking

Leaving the mines, the track continues down and eventually fords Little Tongue Gill near the confluence of Little Tongue and Tongue Gill. It then follows the wall down to the road at Mill Bridge; which lies just north of the Traveller's Rest Inn. We now face a road walk of about a mile back to the startpoint. On a hot day a stop off at the Traveller's Rest to rehydrate is difficult to resist.

Route 6   Alcock Tarn from Grasmere (a circular route) Total climbing about 1000 ft (304m), 3 miles (5 km).

This short walk is never the less quite taxing and gives excellent views of the mountains to the west of Grasmere. Park your car in Grasmere, wherever you can find space, and take the minor road which leads past Dove Cottage. This climbs for about one quarter of a mile to the summit of How Top, where there is a seat beside the road. A gravelled track bears off to the left at this point signposted 'Public Footpath Alcock Tarn.' Follow the track up the hillside as far as the gate but do not go through it. Instead take the rough path to the right of the wall enclosing the wood. Follow the wall up onto the fell where the track becomes enclosed between two substantial walls with even more substantial pillared gateways set in them. These constructions seem curiously out of place in such a remote area bounding, as they do, such a minor track. As you climb higher the views to the west gradually improve, revealing more of the Langdales and beyond. The path continues to follow the wall until a gap appears, through which you may pass to the tarn. The tarn has been dammed at its southern end and has obviously been used as a water supply in the past. On a fine day Alcock Tarn**(U)** is an ideal place for a picnic with plenty of open space for youngsters. The whole area is National Trust owned and is criss-crossed by many paths. The old ruined building, set into the hillside just west of the tarn, is possibly the site of Michael's farmstead which was made famous by Wordsworth in his poem 'Michael' (The Shepherd of Greenhead Gill) **(LH9)**.

Alcock Tarn with Windermere beyond

The Helvellyn Range
Walking

To return to Grasmere continue north along the tarn into the narrow defile that overlooks Greenhead Gill. The path drops steeply down into the gill to join the path from the Swan Hotel (described in **Route 5**). Notice that on the 1:25000 map, the woodland adjacent to the path is still called 'Michael's Fold.'

Route 7 Alcock Tarn from Rydal.

Return by Heron Pike-Nab Scar Ridge. Total climbing about 1800 ft (548 m), 5 miles (8 km)

This alternative route has the advantage of a beautiful low level path from Rydal to Grasmere as well as the physical stimulation of attaining a respectable height on the Fairfield Horseshoe Ridge. The startpoint is the cul de sac which leads to Rydal Hall and Rydal Mount **(W)**. There is usually parking space on the left side of the road, except when there is a church service in progress. Walk up the road past Rydal Mount to the point where the road branches to the left. Here a sign indicates the public footpath to Grasmere. Pass through the gate and follow the path west through wood and parkland as it contours round the lower slopes of Nab Scar. As you walk you will get glimpses through the trees of the busy main road below, carrying busloads of tourists to Grasmere, and

> A professor of physics at Rydal
> Would maintain the lakes were all tidal,
> And to this he adhered,
> Though the scientists jeered
> And assured him his theories were idle.
> Lakeland Limericks, Gibbs,1942

feel relieved that you are up here in relative peace and solitude. The large stone wall set into the hillside, which you encounter along the route, is part of the Thirlmere aqueduct which occasionally appears above ground as it negotiates a ravine. The aqueduct in this area was built by the cut and fill method and the observant eye can identify its course from time to time. Eventually the path emerges from the parkland to join the minor road from Grasmere to 'How Top.' Follow the directions in **Route 6** from this point to Alcock Tarn.

The return route from the tarn follows **Route 6** into Greenhead Gill but then turn east and follow the steep winding path which climbs up to the summit of Heron Pike from the bend in Greenhead Gill. From Heron Pike just follow the ridge path south back towards Rydal. As you descend take in the views of Ambleside with Windermere beyond. Esthwaite Water and Coniston Water can also be seen from here.

Rydal Mount (circa 1900)

Carlisle Library

The Helvellyn Range
Walking

As can be seen from the maps in the centre pages, the foregoing walk descriptions do not cover all of the possible walks on these fells. The walks described are designed to enable one to end up where one started with a minimum amount of road walking involved. Lower level walks are also included for those who do not wish to ascend 2000ft+ every day. With two vehicles the permutations are more numerous. A walk from Clough Head at the north of the map, for example, finishing up at Rydal in the south would make a very long and satisfying day for the enthusiast who is happy to complete a route of 15 miles (24 km) with about 5200ft (1584m) of climbing.

A popular full day route is the Fairfield Round or Horseshoe. To avoid unnecessary road walking on the busy road between Ambleside and Rydal the route is best tackled from Ambleside, rather than Rydal.

Route 8 - Fairfield Round - starting and finishing in Ambleside.
Total climbing 2660 ft (810 m), 9 miles (14 km).

From the centre of Ambleside make your way to Rothay Park, past the cinema, church and primary school. Walk through the park to the west, crossing the River Rothay by the footbridge, and turn right onto the back road between Clappersgate and Rydal. This is a much safer and a more pleasant walk than following the main road between Ambleside and Rydal. This quiet road emerges onto the main road just west of Rydal Bridge. Turn left onto the footpath at the side of the road for about 300m to reach the road up to Rydal Hall and Rydal Mount. Carefully cross over here and walk up past the church and Rydal Mount to joint the footpath leading up onto the ridge of Nab Scar. From here it is a steady and steep ascent to the summit of Heron Pike, followed by a more gentle stroll along the rest of the ridge towards the summit of Fairfield itself. Fine views are to be had in all directions from this elevated ridge. The route bears right at the head of the valley before the summit of Fairfield is reached, but most will want to visit the summit before crossing Rydal Head to Hart Crag and beginning the return half of the walk. In misty conditions follow the advice given under **Route 2** (on page 10) for finding your way off Fairfield. From Hart Crag follow the ridge path southeastwards which initially descends and then rises again to reach the cairn on Dove Crag. From here take the path due south which descends gradually to the summit of High Pike and then more steeply down to Low Pike. The path follows a drystone wall, keeping to the apex of the ridge for most of the way. Before Nook End Farm the path turns left to cross the Scandale Beck by a road bridge. The rest of the route is via the farm access road which gradually descends into Ambleside to emerge at the foot of Kirkstone Road.

The Helvellyn Range
Local History

1. Dalton Sir John, Ascents of Helvellyn

Sir John Dalton; Father of Atomic Theory, born at Eaglesfield, near Cockermouth, ascended Helvellyn annually for forty years. His motives were partly to make meteorological observations and partly, as he expressed it, "to bring into exercise a set of muscles which would otherwise have grown stiff." Apparently on one occasion, when caught in a thick mist, he and his companions were trying to grope their way down the mountain holding on to each others coat tails. Suddenly the doctor stopped, exclaiming "Not one step more! There is nothing but mist to tread on!" When the mist cleared they found themselves on the edge of the cliff directly above Red Tarn. It is perhaps a pity that the unfortunate Charles Gough did not have a similar premonition when he journeyed over Helvellyn in 1805. (See below; Monuments of Helvellyn).

2. Echoes of Ullswater

A visitor attraction of the eighteenth century at Ullswater was to 'try the echoes.' Vessels on the lake were armed with swivel guns and on a still evening, it was said, twenty five distant reverberations could be heard from the discharge of a swivel with only two ounces of powder. Mr Hutchinson in his 'Excursion to the Lakes,' page 65, gives the following description of such an event having landed on the shores of a bay opposite Watermillock."Whilst we sat to regale, the barge put off from shore to a station where the finest echoes were to be obtained from the surrounding mountains. The vessel was provided with six brass cannon, mounted on swivels. On discharging one of these pieces, the report was echoed from the opposite rocks, where, by reverberation, it seemed to roll from cliff to cliff, and return through every cave and valley, till the decreasing tumult gradually died away upon the ear." The practice was continued in more recent times. Behind the Patterdale Hotel is a crag known at one time as Nell Crag. In the eighteen thirties a cannon was occasionally fired from here to the great delight of the visitors.

The Sheep of Lakeland

The Herdwick is a small, hardy breed, ideally suited to the harsh conditions encountered in the Cumbrian mountains. According to legend their ancestors were the survivors of a flock which were washed up on the Cumberland coast from a wrecked Spanish Galleon. Another story attributes their introduction to the Vikings, who imported them from Scandinavia, when they settled here. Whatever their ancestry they are a true hill breed and very resistant to the local climate, which is persistently wet and cold. The Herdwicks form a real and lasting attachment to their native fell or 'heaf' and will return year after year to the same grazing ground. According to a local farmer the sheep are instinctive survivors. In a blizzard they will collect at the ridge ends as they seem to know that the wind will blow the snow off these places. They avoid hollows where the snow will cover them up. A lot of them make for the farm! (Wouldn't you??)

3. Greenside Mine Disasters

In its long life Greenside Mine only suffered two major accidents, both occurring towards the end of the mine's life. The first of these was due to a fire which started in the north shaft over the weekend causing carbon monoxide to diffuse into the workings. On Monday 7th July 1952 a group of miners were driven back by strong fumes as they approached the lift shaft, but not before hearing the shouts of miner Leo Mulyran, who had already descended to the bottom of the shaft. In the subsequent attempt to rescue him three men died, as did Mulyran himself. The heroic rescue attempt was recognised by justly deserved medals and commendations. The second fatal accident occurred in 1960 when the mine was about to close. The Atomic Energy Authority arranged to explode two charges of TNT, one of 500 lbs and the other of 250 lbs, in order to conduct seismic tests. The data was needed to calibrate instruments which would be used to monitor underground nuclear explosions. The charges were fired electrically from the surface but only the larger one went off. After the explosion the mine was ventilated and declared safe but two men, who later went in, were asphyxiated by an isolated pocket of gas trapped in one of the stopes. At the time the secrecy surrounding the project, and the involvement of the Atomic Energy Authority, led to rumours that a small atomic bomb had been exploded in the mine.

Left: Greenside Mine in the 1990's

Helvellyn (Hill of Willan?)
another explanation of the name:

the hill that forms the wall
or defence of the lake'.

This derives from the Norse Hel - Hill, Gival - Well, and Lyn - Lake. Literally this could be 'The hill containing the lake which is like a well.'

4. Keppel Cove Dam Flood

At 1.30 a.m. on Saturday, 29th October 1927, after a period of exceptional rainfall, the earthen wall of Keppel Cove Tarn Dam burst, causing a great wall of water to descend on Glenridding far below. The size of the deluge was such that it left a gap in the dam 80ft wide by 60ft deep. The flood rushed down Glenridding Beck carrying away Rattlebeck bridge, flooding houses alongside the beck and Eagle Farm to a depth of five to six feet. Debris, including dead sheep and a tea hut, was deposited on the other side of the lake near Side Farm. The basement bedrooms of the Glenridding Hotel were flooded and four sleeping girls floated up to the ceiling on their mattresses. One of these had a near escape as she was swept through a window but was then saved by one Ernest Thompson. The peninsula at Glenridding, which is now the site of the steamer pier, was formed as a result of this flood which also brought down a mass of large rocks with it. The rocks were used to build up this strip of land which is now a popular recreation area for visitors.

The Keppel Cove earth dam was replaced by a rough concrete dam which also burst, but less spectacularly, in 1931. The second dam is still to be seen complete with large hole in the base.

5. King Dunmail and Dunmail Raise

"That pile of stones heaped over brave Dunmail's bones
He who had my supreme command
Last king of rocky Cumberland"

Wordsworth's 'Waggoner'

The story of King Dunmail and his last battle at Dunmail Raise in the year 945 is steeped in Arthurean legend. There are several versions of the story, some more fanciful than others. The description here is a compilation of these.

Dunmail was the son of Owain, one of the strongest of the Cumbrian kings who came to the throne about 920. Owain was descended from the old Caesarian line of the kings of Strathclyde, who by this time had lost much of their power and influence due to attacks from Anglian invaders, who encroached into the Scottish lowlands. Owain ruled his kingdom from Penrith as Carlisle had been sacked by the Danes in 876 and was a ruin. The seven tombs forming the

Keppel Cove and Dams
(from the Helvellyn ridge above Brown Cove)

The Helvellyn Range
Local History

'Giant's Grave' and the 'Giant's Thumb' in Penrith churchyard date back to this time and indicate that Penrith was an important centre. The popular tradition which says that the monuments are the tomb of a giant, 'Hugh or Owen Caesarius,' probably records some dim memory of Owain. Minstrels through the ages might have sung of Owain as a *great man* even *a giant of a man.'* It would be quite easy for such a ballad to become associated with the obelisks in the churchyard, which might have been then seen as the grave of this '*giant.'*

Owain, together with his uncle, King Constantine II of the Scots, plotted with the Vikings of Galloway and the Isles against the English King Athelstan, to whom they had previously sworn allegiance as King of all Britain. This led to a great battle on the flat topped mountain near Ecclefechan in Galloway, called Burnswark, at which the English were victorious. What happened to Owain after the battle is not recorded, but Dunmail, his son and successor, apparently did not learn from this experience. Dunmail continued his dangerous alliance with the Vikings of Galloway and the Isles. King Edmund, the Saxon king, who succeeded Athelstan on the English throne, was quick to act, sending an army across Stainmore which defeated Dunmail at a place unknown. After this battle, Edmund, with the usual barbarity of the times, put out the eyes of Dunmail's two sons and gave his country to Malcolm; King of Scotland, on condition he preserved peace in the northern parts of England. Although several sites for the battle have been suggested, including Orrest Head at Windermere, legend and popular belief portray Dunmail Raise as the battleground. The story of the battle is interwoven with legend and superstition but is a fine tale to hear. I quote from an account given in **1927 in 'Cycling' magazine by one W.T. Palmer.**

The Cairn on Dunmail Raise

"The Raise has legend of one mighty battle a thousand years ago. King Edmund the Saxon was quelling the raider Britons on his border, and Dunmail of Cumberland came in for punitive attention. The armies met on this level among the hills, and a formless pile of stones marks the burial place of those who fell. Here is a pretty legend: The crown of Dunmail of Cumberland was charmed, giving its wearer a succession in his kingdom. Therefore King Edmund the Saxon coveted it above all things. When Dunmail came to the throne of the mountain land a wizard in Gilsland Forest held a master

charm to defeat the promise of his crown. He Dunmail slew. The magician was able to make himself invisible save at cock crow and to destroy him the hero braved a cordon of wild wolves at night. At the first peep of dawn, he entered the cave where the wizard was lying. Leaping to his feet the magician called out "Where river runs north or south with the storm," ere Dunmail's sword silenced him.

The story came to the ear of the covetous Saxon, who, after much enquiry of his priests, found that an incomplete curse, although powerful against Dunmail, could scarcely hurt another holder of the crown. Spies were accordingly sent into Cumbria to find where a battle could be fought favourable to the magician's words. On Dunmail Raise, in times of storm even in unromantic today, the torrent sets north or south in capricious fashion. The spies found the place, found also fell land chiefs who were persuaded to become secret allies of the Saxon. The campaign began. Dunmail moved his army south to meet the invader, and they joined battle in the pass. For long hours the battle was with the Cumbrians; the Saxons were driven down the hill again and again. As his foremost tribes became exhausted, Dunmail retired and called on his reserves - they were mainly the ones favouring the southern king. On they came, spreading in well - armed lines from side to side of the hollow way, but instead of opening to let the weary warriors through, they delivered an attack on them. Surprised, the army reeled back and their rear was attacked with redoubled violence by the Saxons. The loyal ranks were forced to stand back to back round their king; assailed by superior forces they fell rapidly, and ere long the brave chief was shot down by a traitor of his own bodyguard:

'My crown," cried he, " bear it away; never let the Saxon flaunt it.'

A few stalwarts took the charmed treasure from his hands, and with a furious onslaught made the attackers give way. Step by step they fought their way up the ghyll of Dunmail's beck - broke through all resistance on the open fell, and, aided by a dense cloud, evaded their pursuers. Two hours later the faithful few met by Grisedale Tarn, and consigned the crown to its depths - "till Dunmail come again to lead us." And every year the warriors come back, draw up the magic circlet from the depths of the wild mountain tarn, and carry it with them over Seat Sandal to where the king is sleeping his age long sleep. They knock with his spear on the topmost stone of the cairn and from its heart comes a voice:

"Not yet; not yet - wait a while my warriors."

The cairn can still be seen in the central reservation on the summit of Dunmail Raise. Another legend says that Dunmail did not die in the battle; that he survived for thirty years in Strathclyde and died a pilgrim in Rome. Be that as it may, Edmund did not gain a successor for his throne. Four years after the battle on Dunmail Raise he was assassinated, and his kingdom went into ruin."

6. Memorials of Helvellyn

There are three memorials on Helvellyn:

(i) The first of these is encountered as one crosses Striding Edge. A white painted iron plaque marks the spot where Robert Dixon of Rookings, Patterdale, died on 27th May 1858, while following the Patterdale Foxhounds.

(ii) The second memorial, which stands on the summit plateau of Helvellyn directly above Red Tarn, records an event that has since become famous through the attentions of the Lakeland poets. A large memorial stone, set into a cairn, records the death of Charles Gough of Manchester who perished in the spring of 1805 when attempting to cross from Patterdale to Wythburn. A fall of snow had partially obscured the path and he apparently fell from the head of Red Cove onto the rocks below. His dog, which accompanied him on that fateful day, remained with the body until it was found three months later by William Harrison of Hartsop. It was this act of extreme devotion which captured the imagination of both Wordsworth and Scott. Scott's verses on 'Helvellyn' refer to the event and below Wordsworth's 'Fidelity' tells the tale in full:-

1. A barking sound the shepherd hears,
A cry as of a dog or fox;
He halts and searches with his eyes,
Among the scattered rocks:
And now at distance can discern
A stirring in a brake or fern;
And instantly a dog is seen,
Glancing through that covert green.

2. The dog is not of mountain breed;
Its motions, too, are wild and shy;
With something, as the shepherd thinks,
Unusual in its cry:
Nor is there anyone in sight
All round, in hollow or on height;
Nor shout, nor whistle strikes his ear:
What is the creature doing here?

3. It was a cove, a huge recess,
That keeps, till June December's snow;
A lofty precipice in front,
A silent tarn below !
Far in the bosom of Helvellyn,
Remote from public road or dwelling,
Pathway, or cultivated land;
From trace of human foot or hand.

4. There sometimes doth a leaping fish
Send through the tarn a lonely cheer;
The crags repeat the raven's croak,
In sympathy austere;
Thither the rainbow comes - the cloud -
And mists that spread the flying shroud;
And sunbeams; and the sounding blast,
That if it could, would hurry past;
But that enormous barrier binds it fast.

5. Not free from boding thoughts, a while
The shepherd stood; then makes his way
Towards the dog, o'er rocks and stones,
As quickly as he may;
Not far had gone before he found
A human skeleton on the ground;
The appalled discoverer with a sigh
Looks round to learn the history.

6. From those abrupt and perilous rocks
The man had fallen, that place of fear!
At length upon the shepherds mind
It breaks, and all is clear:
He instantly recalled the name,
And who he was, and whence he came;
Remembered, too, the very day
On which the traveller passed this way.

7. But hear a wonder, for whose sake
This lamentable tale I tell!
A lasting monument of words
This wonder merits well.
The dog which still was hovering nigh,
Repeating the same timid cry,
This dog had been through three month's space
A dweller in that savage place.

8. Yes, proof was plain that since the day,
When this ill-fated traveller died,
The dog had watched about the spot,
Or by his master's side:
How nourished here through such long time
He knows who gave that love sublime:
And gave that strength of feeling great
Above all human estimate.

Charles Gough's remains are buried at Tirril between Pooley Bridge and Penrith. There is speculation how the dog, a terrier bitch named Foxey, survived for three months on the mountain. Some say the dog fed on rabbits, or sheep, or stray birds. But one thing is certain, the flesh on the man's legs was completely eaten and nothing left but the bones.

Canon Rawnsley in his book *'Literary Associations of the English Lakes'* disputes the suggestion that Foxey ate the remains of her master. He quotes a letter dated Yanwath 30th of Eighth month 1805 which contains a brief note of the incident. In that letter, written only six months after the event, it is stated that 'his bones were bleached white though covered with his clothes, and his skull was separated and found at a distance from the rest. --- *His faithful dog had attended his relics between three and four months, but how it had subsisted itself is difficult to suppose, though it appeared to the people who collected his remains that **'it eat grass.'** Foxey gave birth to pups during her vigil which were found dead. Further evidence says Rawnsley that Foxey survived only on grass and carrion mutton which did not provide enough sustenance to support her pups.

John Gough's Memorial Stone
on the summit of Helvellyn

(iii) The third memorial on Helvellyn is to be found a hundred yards or so south of the summit shelter beside the path leading towards Wythburn. A recently re-erected plaque records the first landing of an aircraft on the summit of an English mountain. On the 22nd December 1926, pilots John Leeming and Bert Hinkler landed an Avro 585 Gosport aeroplane on the summit plateau. After a short stay they then flew back to Woodford in Cheshire. (Woodford is very near the present Manchester Airport).

The Helvellyn Range
Local History

7. Thirlmere and Manchester
In 1894 Thirlmere had the dubious distinction of being the first lake in the district to be converted into a reservoir by Manchester Corporation. Prior to the building of the dam, Thirlmere, formerly known as Leathes Water or Wythburn Water, consisted of two parts connected by a narrow and shallow channel. The hamlet of Armboth on the west side was connected by a bridge over this channel to Dale Head Park and the Keswick road. Armboth or 'City,' as it was known to the lead miners of Helvellyn, was to disappear for ever with the raising of the water level. Manchester had originally wanted to extract water from Ullswater but, due to local opposition, they were diverted from this course and eventually settled on Thirlmere where there were fewer influential landowners to deal with. One other problem with Ullswater was the presence of Greenside Lead Mine. It was incorrectly supposed that the lead workings would contaminate the lake water. Similar fears at Thirlmere led to the closing of Helvellyn Mine in 1880. The later schemes at Haweswater and Ullswater were required to blend in with the natural environment and not to alter the natural beauty of the area. The Thirlmere scheme, however, was not bound by such tight constraints. As a result, for many years access was denied to the lake and visitors were discouraged. Unsightly notices prohibiting trespass on water board land were commonly encountered. Happily this is no longer the situation. The signs have disappeared and North West Water has constructed paths and stiles giving easy access to the lake and the surrounding woods. Thirlmere will, however, never look a natural lake. Its height goes up and down with the season and the demand for water. At times of drought the exposed white rocky shores contrast sharply with the conifer forest above, emphasising that it is no longer a natural lake. Whatever one thinks of the spoiling of the area by these 19th century engineers, one can only admire their vision and engineering skills. The aqueduct that carries Thirlmere's water the 96 miles to Manchester is a series of tunnels, buried channels and pipelines which utilise gravity alone to keep the water moving.

8. Brownrigg Well
If the weather is fine, and you have time to linger, you may wish to visit Brownrigg Well in order to slake your thirst or refill your water bottle. The well is the source of the small stream which emerges from the hillside about three hundred feet below and three hundred yards due west of the trig. point on the summit. This stream runs down into Whelpside Gill. However, in the last century, the water from the well was diverted north and down into Mines Gill, where it helped provide water power for Helvellyn Mine. All traces of the dam have gone but the 'leat' which led the water north is still visible as a narrow groove in the hillside.

Mr H Wilkinson of Penrith, writing in Cumbria Magazine in 1954 at the grand old age of 90, described how, in his younger days around 1900-1910, he always stopped at the well to partake of its icy cold water. At that time there was an iron cup, fixed by a chain, provided for the thirsty walker. Regrettably, as you might expect, the cup is no longer there.

9. The Shepherd of Greenhead Ghyll

This pathetic tale is related by Wordsworth in his poem 'Michael,' which is too long to reproduce in full here. I will relate a brief synopsis of the tale: Long ago a shepherd called Michael was married to a wife, Isabel, twenty years his junior. They were blessed late in life with an only son called Luke. From the age of ten Luke worked with his father, who was then sixty six, day in and day out. In the evening they would rest in their cottage which was high on the side of Greenhead Ghyll and could be seen from Grasmere and the surrounding vale. Every night Isabel lit a lamp to see them home which, as it stood in the window of the cottage, could be seen by the whole valley. This light became famous and was named 'The Evening Star' by the residents of Grasmere Vale.

Dove Cottage, Grasmere (from an old guide book)

Unfortunately, due to the misfortune of his brother's son who failed in business, Michael, who had agreed to be bound in surety for his nephew, had to give up half of his living to cover the debt. The farm could no longer support both he and his son. Luke, who was eighteen years old at this time, had to leave and live with a relative in the city who agreed to try and find work for the lad. Before Luke left, his father and he laid the foundations of a new sheepfold beside the ghyll which, Michael promised, would be ready for his son's return, when his fortune was made. While his son was away Michael added to the sheepfold in his spare moments, ever looking forward to Luke's eventual return. Alas it was not to be. Luke soon became influenced by city life and turned to drink, gambling and coarse living. The old man lost heart when he heard the news and realised that Luke was not coming back. Michael finally died at the age of ninety one, with the sheepfold still unfinished. Isobel survived a further few years before the estate was sold and went into a stranger's hand.

Wordsworth relates how the cottage which was named the 'Evening Star' has gone, a ploughshare has been through the ground on which it stood. Yet the oak is left that grew beside the door. A possible site for the cottage is immediately west of Alcock Tarn where the remains of a house built into the hillside is to be seen. A few yards further down the slope to the right of the cottage are the rotten remains of a large tree stump. The view from this point is just as the poem describes, encompassing Grasmere Vale, Easedale and Dunmail Raise.

10. Wordsworth - the brothers' parting stone

The inscribed stone which stands just off the path, a short distance east of Grisedale Tarn, marks the spot where William bade goodbye to his brother John for the last time. William would see his brother on his way, accompanying him as far as Grisedale Tarn. Unfortunately, shortly after this last parting, John was to perish in the loss of his ship, the East Indiaman, the *'Earl of Abergavenny.'* On Friday night, February 5th 1805 the ship was wrecked on The Shambles, off the Portland Bill, through the incompetency of the pilot. Wordsworth records this sad happening in a poem of lament, composed at the parting stone. There follows a short excerpt :

Wordsworth s Grave in Grasmere Churchyard

Carlisle Library

> The sheep boy whistled loud and lo!
> That instant, startled by the shock,
> The buzzard mounted from the rock
> Deliberate and slow:
> Lord of the air, he took his flight:
> Oh! could he on that woeful night
> Have lent his wing, my brother dear,
> For one poor moment's space to thee
>
> And all who struggled with the sea
> When safety was so near.
>
> *III*
>
> Here did we stop and here look round,
> While each into himself descends,
> For that last thought of parting friends
> That is not to be found.......

Queen of the Mountains

Helvellyn and her companions while not exactly within the inner sanctum are yet not subsidiary to Scafell. If Scafell is thought of as the King of the Lake mountains, then Helvellyn is more like the Queen than the Prince. (Perhaps burly Skiddaw, the only other peak to over - top 3,000 ft. is the Prince). She is of equal importance with King Scafell in the general scheme and below her spreads like a train the beautiful lake of Ullswater. She is more accessible, too, as a Queen should be, than Scafell, and on her Striding edge, that famous dizzy walk, she offers the adventurous tourist the slightly spurious thrill of a danger that looks greater than it is ....

E.F. Bozman, The English Countryside (1939)

The Helvellyn Range
A Selected Bibliography used in the Historical Research for this Series of Books

Title	Author	Year
A Study of Hartsop Valley	LDSPB	1976
A History of Man in the Lake District	Rollinson	1967
A Thousand Miles of Wandering in the Border Country	Bogg	1898
Beauty of Buttermere (Novel in three volumes)	Cruickshank	1841
Beneath the Lakeland Fells	Cumbria Amenity Trust	1992
Bluebirds	Campbell Gina	1968
Bye Ways in Lakeland	W T Palmer	1952
Chronicles of Patterdale	Little (W.I.)	1952
Coniston	Collingwood	1900
Country Life Magazine	October	1972
Crag and Hound in Lakeland	Benson	1902
Cumberland and Westmorland Antiquarian and Archaeological Society Transactions		
Cumbria Magazine	Dalesman	
Description of Lakes	Penny Magazine	1837
Descriptive Guide to the Lakes	Otley	1850
Descriptive Tour and Guide to the Lakes	Housman J.	1802
Dry Stone Walls	Garner L.	1984
English Lakes	Atkinson	1853
English Lakes	Martineau H.	1855
Fell days	Sutton G.	1948
Fortnight s Ramble to the Lakes	Budworth J.	1792
Gossiping Guide to Shap and Haweswater	Partington	1923
Guide to Lakes	Aust Mrs M.	1810
Guide to Lakes	Robinson	1819
Guide to Lakes	West T.	1799
Heart of Lakeland	Oppenheimer L. J.	1908
History of Cumberland	Hutchinson	1794
Kelton and Knockmurton Iron Mines	Hewer R.	1988
Lakeland and the Border Counties Vol 1 - 3 (Articles from the Cumberland News in the 1930 s)	Mc Intyre	
Lakeland Limericks	Gibbs	1942
Legends and Historical Notes of North Westmorland	Gibson	1887
Life of John Hatfield, the Keswick Impostor	Scott & Benson	1846
Literary Associations of the English Lakes	Rawnsley	1894
Memories of Dunmail Raise (Article in Cycling Magazine)	Palmer	1937
Mines of the Lake District Fells	Adams J.	1988
Mountain Ascents	Barrow John	1886
Observations during a tour of the Lakes	Radcliffe Mrs A	1795
Penny Magazine	July	1837
Pictorial Guide to the Lakeland Fells	Wainwright	1966-1992
Place Names of Cumberland		1940
Ratty	Gowan W.M.	1947
Records of Patterdale	Morris W P	1903
Royal Observer Corps Journal	Thomson	Feb-1988
Ruskin and Brantwood	Whitehouse	1937
Scawfell Pike, the ascent of	Hudson	1851
Survey of the Lakes	Clarke J.	1789
The Lakes	Sanderson	1807
The Old Man - Ravings and Ramblings	Gibson	1849
Thoughts on the Parish of Caldbeck	Pool	1862
Windscale Works	UKAEA	1966
Wordsworth s Scenery of the Lakes of England	Hudson J	1853

The Legend of Aira Force

Aira Force is the scene of a sad yet romantic legend. In the far-off centuries there dwelt at the tower adjoining the Force a beautiful lady named Emma, betrothed to a famed knight (Sir Eglamore), who had long been engaged in war in Eastern lands. His long absence had affected her health and she wandered in her sleep by the bank of the torrent at night, dreaming of her lover. It was here the knight found her when he returned unexpectedly. When he touched her she suddenly awoke from sleep and fell down the deep precipice into the water. The knight leaped into the torrent to rescue her. She opened her eyes and recognised him before she died. The heartbroken man built a cell near the Falls where he dwelt in solitude.

Edmund Bogg 1898

The Helvellyn Range
A Selection of other Titles available from P3 Publications

Coast to Coast - in the middle ages! Lesley Bell
These were the parting words from Eric's eighty eight year old mum on their visit to her just before setting out on the coast to coast walk. Considering that Lesley and Eric did the walk in what was to prove to be just about the wettest October in living memory, her words rang true more than once. This book is not a guide to the Coast to Coast walk, it is a humorous account of the experiences of one middle aged couple who did the walk in October 1998. Lesley describes the trials, the tribulations and the pleasures of the walk; including the many friends they made en-route. Lesley's narrative is littered with examples of her West Yorkshire wit which kept their spirits up and will keep the reader chuckling from page to page. The book gives a realistic view of the experiences that one might expect to counter when tackling the walk in less than perfect weather conditions.
ISBN 0 9537203 3 0 A5 format, 64 pages, perfect bound, 37 photographs, 9 drawings, (£4.99)

Halkidiki Walking - Wandern - 20 walks in the green garden of Greece, 20 Wanderungen im gr nen Garten Griechenlands, **David Ramshaw** -   Dual Language edition - German translation from the English by Kallia Kotsovolos. A brand new walking guide for the new millenium! This dual language English/German guide gives detailed information on 20 walking routes of varying length and difficulty covering the whole of Halkidiki. There are 6 routes in Kassandra, 6 routes in Sithonia, 3 routes in Athos and 5 routes in the Holomondas mountains. **ISBN 0 9522098 9 6 (Price in UK £6.99)** 128 pages in full colour, with 20 3D type maps and profile graphs as well as over 70 full colour photographs. Published April 2000 by the Halkidiki Hotel Owners Association.

Three Ridings on Foot - A walk around the Yorkshire Border Authors: Ann and Geoffrey Birch, Joyce and Derek Hellawell, Wilfrid Kennedy, John Lieberg, Paul Widger, Mary and Albert Willis.
This book describes a 706 km (438 mile walk) utilising public rights of way and permissive paths on and around the Yorkshire border. It has been compiled from current Ordnance Survey pathfinder and Outdoor Leisure maps by a group of friends who are regular walkers. The walk is divided into 34 sections which give accurate route descriptions. Appendices provide information on distances, maps, tourist information centres and youth hostels. 200 mm by 100 mm, 120 pages, sewn, 28 illustrations **ISBN 0 99522098 4 5   (£2.99)**

To order any of these books: phone / write **D. Ramshaw**, 13 Beaver Road, Carlisle, Cumbria, CA2 7PS, England U.K. telephone: 01228 543302; Ordering details on website: **http://www.p3publications.com.** (More books on website) Books can also be ordered through any bookshop by quoting the appropriate ISBN.